GW00859506

Properties of Materials

Stiff or Bendy

Our Lady's Catholic Infant School

Charlotte Guillain

Heinemann
LIBRARY

www.heinemannlibrary.co.uk
Visit our website to find out more information about Heinemann Library books.

To order:
☎ Phone +44 (0) 1865 888066
📄 Fax +44 (0) 1865 314091
💻 Visit www.heinemannlibrary.co.uk

Heinemann is an imprint of Capstone Global Library Limited, a company incorporated in England and Wales having its registered office at 7 Pilgrim Street, London, EC4V 6LB – Registered company number: 6695582

"Heinemann" is a registered trademark of Pearson Education Limited, under licence to Capstone Global Library Limited

Text © Capstone Global Library Limited 2009
First published in hardback in 2009
The moral rights of the proprietor have been asserted.

Edited by Charlotte Guillain and Catherine Veitch
Designed by Joanna Hinton-Malivoire
Picture research by Elizabeth Alexander
Originated by Heinemann Library
Printed by South China Printing Company Limited

ISBN 978 0 431 19351 9 (hardback)
13 12 11 10 09
10 9 8 7 6 5 4 3 2 1

British Library Cataloguing in Publication Data
Guillain, Charlotte
Stiff or bendy. – (Properties of materials)
530.4
A full catalogue record for this book is available from the British Library.

Acknowledgements
The author and publishers are grateful to the following for permission to reproduce copyright material:
Alamy pp. 15 (© Geri Lavrov), 20 (© Helene Rogers), 23 **bottom** (© Geri Lavrov); © Capstone Publishers p. 22 (Karon Dubke); Corbis p. 21 (© Reuters); Getty Images pp. 11 (Jae Rew/Riser), 17 (Penny Tweedie), 18 (Carl D. Walsh/Aurora); iStockphoto p. 13; Photolibrary pp. 4, 23 **middle bottom** (Inaki Antonana/age footstock), 5 (Pomerantz Rich/Botanica), 7 (Image Source), 14 (Pierre Bourrier); Shutterstock pp. 6 (© Tomasz Parys), 8 (© Peter Baxter), 9 (© Emin Ozkan), 10, 23 **top** (© Monkey Business Images), 12, 23 middle top (© Istvan Csak), 16 (© Stephen Aaron Rees), 19 (© Rannev).

Cover photograph of a garden hose reproduced with permission of Photolibrary (Digital Vision/Thomas Barwick). Back cover photograph of someone folding paper reproduced with permission of Shutterstock (© Rannev).

The publishers would like to thank Nancy Harris and Adriana Scalise for their assistance in the preparation of this book.

Every effort has been made to contact copyright holders of any material reproduced in this book. Any omissions will be rectified in subsequent printings if notice is given to the publisher.

Contents

Stiff materials

Some things are stiff.

Stiff things can be hard.

Stiff things cannot bend.

Stiff things cannot stretch.

Bendy materials

Some things are bendy.

Bendy things can be hard or soft.

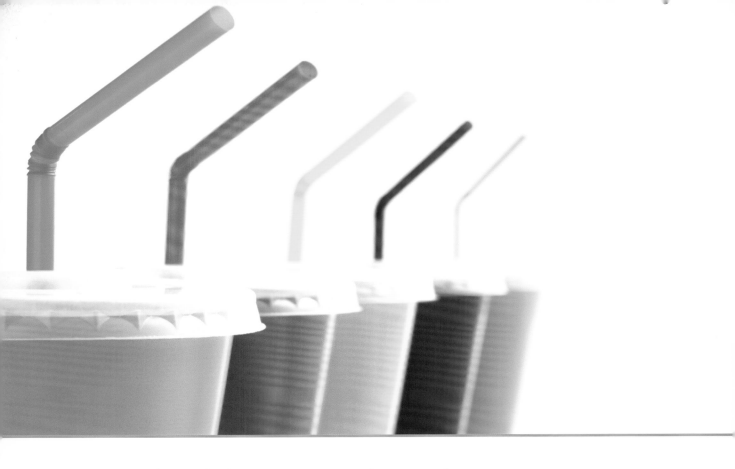

Bendy things can bend.

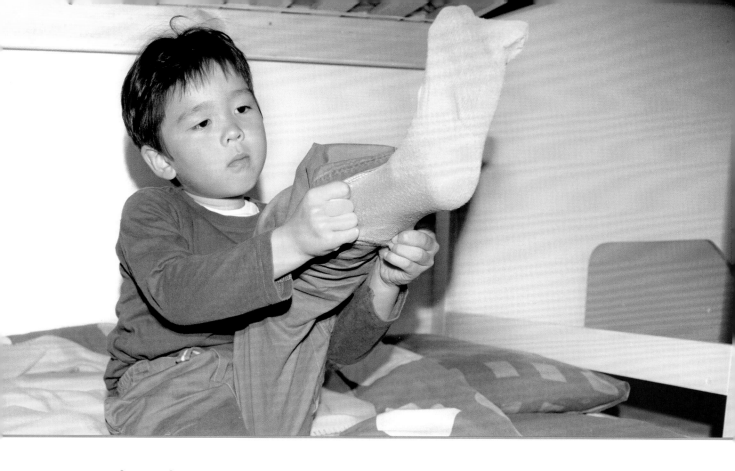

Bendy things can stretch.

Stiff and bendy materials

Plastic can be stiff.

You cannot bend stiff plastic.

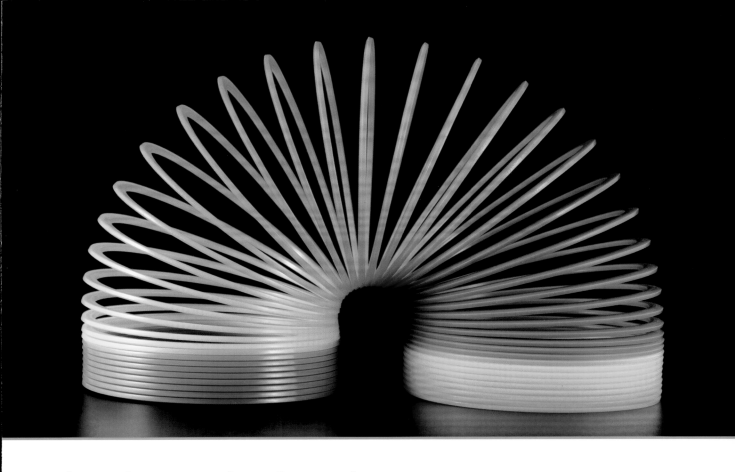

Plastic can be bendy.

You can bend bendy plastic.

Glass is stiff.

You cannot stretch it.

Rubber is bendy.
You can stretch it.

Wood is stiff.

You cannot stretch it.

Wool is bendy.
You can stretch it.

You can tell if something is stiff
or bendy.

You can feel if something is stiff
or bendy.

You can see if something is stiff or bendy.

We can see when things are stiff.

We can see when things are bendy.

Quiz

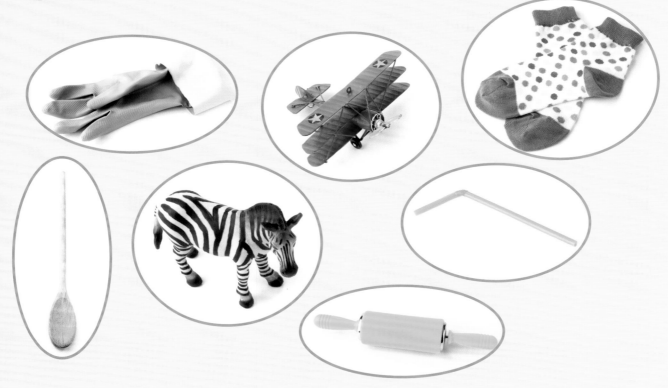

Which of these things are stiff?
Which of these things are bendy?

Picture glossary

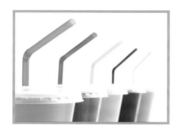
bendy material that can bend without breaking

plastic material that can be soft or hard

stiff hard to bend or move

stretch make something longer or wider, especially by pulling

Index

Note to parents and teachers
Before reading
Tell children that materials can be stiff or bendy. Ask children if they know what "stiff" and "bendy" mean. Pass around several objects and ask children to guess if they are stiff or bendy. Possible objects could be modelling clay, paper, pencil, spoon, scarf, bricks, straw, a glass, and a plastic cup.

After reading
Help children to make an object out of modelling clay. Mix 500 grams of flour and 273 grams of salt in a bowl. Add water (about 237 millilitres) gradually to form a ball. Knead until it no longer falls apart. As children are moulding their clay, ask them if their clay is bendy or stiff. Let their objects dry at room temperature for a couple of days. After they harden, ask the children if they are bendy or stiff. When the clay has completely hardened, let the children paint their objects.